Gardening For Kids

# A Backyard Vegetable Garden For Kids

Amie Jane Leavitt

Mitchell Lane
PUBLISHERS

P.O. Box 196
Hockessin, Delaware 19707
Visit us on the web: www.mitchelllane.com
Comments? email us: mitchelllane@mitchelllane.com

**Mitchell Lane**
**PUBLISHERS**

 # Gardening For Kids

A Backyard Flower Garden for Kids
**A Backyard Vegetable Garden for Kids**
Design Your Own Butterfly Garden
Design Your Own Pond and Water Garden
A Kid's Guide to Container Gardening
A Kid's Guide to Landscape Design
A Kid's Guide to Making a Terrarium
A Kid's Guide to Perennial Gardens
Organic Gardening for Kids

**ABOUT THE AUTHOR:** Amie Jane Leavitt is an
accomplished author and photographer. She
graduated from Brigham Young University as
an education major and has since taught all
subjects and grade levels in both private and
public schools. In addition to teaching, she
has written dozens of books, articles, games,
puzzles, and activity books for kids. She has
traveled the world gathering information for
her writing and capturing beautiful images
with her camera. In fact, she took most of the
photographs used in this book. One of Amie's
favorite hobbies is gardening. She grows her
own vegetables, herbs, and flowers every
year and never tires of watching the tiny
seeds come to life in her garden. Amie hopes
more young people will discover the joys of
gardening and gain a desire to care for the
earth's precious resources. For this particular
book, she'd like to thank her nephew, Isaac,
for assisting with the gardening projects and
agreeing to be photographed.

**PUBLISHER'S NOTE:** The facts on which the story
in this book is based have been thoroughly
researched. Documentation of such research
can be found on page 46. While every possible
effort has been made to ensure accuracy, the
publisher will not assume liability for damages
caused by inaccuracies in the data, and
makes no warranty on the accuracy of the
information contained herein.

**Library of Congress Cataloging-in-Publication
Data**
Leavitt, Amie Jane.
   A backyard vegetable garden for kids / by
Amie Jane Leavitt.
      p. cm. — (Robbie reader. Gardening for
      kids)
   Includes bibliographical references and
index.
   ISBN 978-1-58415-634-5 (library bound)
   1. Vegetable gardening—Juvenile literature.
2. Backyard gardens—Juvenile literature.
I. Title. II. Series.
SB324.L43 2008
635—dc22
                                         2008002244

**Printing**          4    5    6    7    8    9

PLB / PLB2 / PLB2 / PLB2

# Contents

Words in **bold** type can be found in the glossary.

# Introduction

Do you adore plants? If so, you might consider taking up the hobby of vegetable gardening. It's a fun and easy pastime that people of all ages enjoy. You get to spend time outdoors. You get to play in the dirt. You get to watch things grow from tiny seeds into plants. And most importantly, at harvest time, you won't have to buy your vegetables from a grocery store. You'll get to pick basketfuls of fresh produce right from your very own garden. Imagine all of the emerald green leafy lettuces, colorful sweet peppers, crunchy carrots, and juicy vine-ripened tomatoes that you'll get to eat.

The first thing anyone should do when starting a new hobby is take the time to learn all about it. That's why this book was written. Within these pages, you'll discover the basics of vegetable gardening. You'll learn how to find out which vegetables can grow in your area, and at what time of year to plant them. You'll also discover what tools you'll need and how to prepare your garden space. In addition, you'll be given step-by-step instructions for the best way to plant vegetables, from sowing seeds to harvesting the ripened crop. Even if you don't have a yard in which to plant, you'll find out how to grow a variety of vegetables for you and your family.

# What Should I Grow?

The first thing to do when planning a vegetable garden is to decide what to grow. One rule of thumb is simply this: Only grow what you'll eat. If your mother has to bribe you to eat brussels sprouts every time she prepares them for dinner, why would you grow rows and rows of them in your garden? Instead, spend your time and money planting things that you and your family will enjoy eating.

Another basic gardening guideline is to grow the right amount of each type of plant. For example, if you want to eat only a few tomatoes during the summer, planting ten tomato plants would be wasteful. This many plants will produce hundreds of tomatoes—way more than you could possibly eat, even if you had them for every meal all summer long! It would be better to grow only two tomato plants and leave the rest of the garden free for growing other types of vegetables.

Most gardeners love the earth and want to take care of it. They don't believe in wasting its precious resources—and that includes growing more fruits and vegetables than can be used.

Once you understand these basic gardening guidelines, think about the types of vegetables you'd like to grow. Take some time to brainstorm a list. To help get you started, look over the list of vegetables on page 9. Do any of them appeal to you? If not, look in an encyclopedia (en-sy-kloh-PEE-dee-uh) or ask your parents if you can search the Internet for other types of vegetables that you might like to grow.

Once you've made your list, figure out if and when these particular vegetables can be grown in your area. In some areas of the United States, vegetables should be planted in the spring. In other parts of the country, the same vegetables need to be planted in late summer or early fall.

What makes gardening different in one place than in another? The **climate**, or usual weather conditions of a place, determines if and when you can plant certain crops. If the temperature gets too cold or too hot, your plants will die. That's why you have to plant them at the correct time of year. For example, in parts of Arizona, you should not plant crops in the late spring, because summertime temperatures are

## Garden Tip

*Besides growing vegetables, you may want to try growing other **edible** plants called herbs. These plants give special seasonings to food. Some fun herbs to grow include chives, basil, dill, sage, mint, and nasturtium. Not only can you eat the leaves of some herbs, you can also eat their flowers and seeds!*

## Vegetables You Might Like To Grow

| | | |
|---|---|---|
| Beets | Green Beans | Radishes |
| Broccoli | Green Peppers | Spinach |
| Cabbage | Lettuce | Squash |
| Carrots | Onions | Tomatoes |
| Collards | Peas | Turnips |
| Corn | Potatoes | Watermelon |
| Cucumber | Pumpkins | Zucchini |
| Eggplant | | |

generally over 100 degrees F. This would kill most vegetable plants. Instead, gardeners in this area plant their crops in the fall and winter, when temperatures are cooler. It rarely freezes in this part of the country, so vegetable plants can easily grow there in the winter months. Just the opposite is true in northern states, where gardeners have to be more concerned with freezing winter temperatures than they do with hot summer weather.

What type of climate does your area have? When is it best to plant a garden where you live? The easiest way to find the answers to these questions is to visit a garden shop. There you will find all sorts of items related to your new hobby. These shops have books,

*When Isaac visited a garden shop in his city, he took along a notepad and pencil. He looked at the many different seeds for sale. Then he took notes about the vegetables that he wanted to grow in his garden.*

After Isaac studied the seed packets, he decided to buy some tomato plants. There were many different types to choose from. There were salad tomatoes, heirloom tomatoes, beefsteak tomatoes, and lemon boy tomatoes. They all sounded so good that it was really hard for him to decide!

*Isaac asked one of the garden shop employees some questions about the types of vegetables that would be best to grow in his garden. Remember, if you're unsure of anything while at the garden shop, just ask for help.*

plants, seed packets, and wise employees who can answer your questions.

One trick that gardeners use to find out more about a particular vegetable they want to plant is to look at the back of a seed packet. These little envelopes have a whole crop of helpful information. First, the packets describe how to plant the seeds, how much water to give them, and how much sunlight they need. The packets also give information on the various uses for the plant and the different ways to eat the vegetable. At the bottom of each seed packet, you'll see a little map of the United States. Each color on the map represents a **zone** that has its own planting season. Let's say, for example, that you live in the state of Florida, and you want to plant broccoli (see the picture of a broccoli seed packet, page 20). According to the map on the seed packet, you should plant broccoli seeds during the months of July to December. On the other hand, if you live in Utah, you should plant broccoli seeds during the months of April to June.

| # | Type of Vegetable | When to grow in my area |
|---|---|---|
| 1 | | |
| 2 | | |
| 3 | | |
| 4 | | |
| 5 | | |
| 6 | | |
| 7 | | |

While you're at the garden shop, you'll need to look at the seed packets for each type of vegetable that you want to grow. Make a chart like the one above and use it to keep track of the growing season for each vegetable. When you've decided which vegetables will grow best in your area, purchase the seed packets you'll need, and you'll be ready to start gardening.

# Preparing Your Plot

After you've decided which vegetables to plant, you need to gather some tools and prepare your garden space.

Gather the following tools:

**Hoe**—This garden tool has a thin, flat blade that is used for breaking up soil and removing weeds.

**Garden Rake**—This garden tool has a long handle with a row of teeth or prongs at one end. It is used to smooth the soil surface.

**Measuring Tools**—A yardstick and measuring tape can help you determine the proper distance between rows in your garden.

**Hand Trowel or Shovel**—These tools are used to make shallow rows in which the seeds can be planted.

**Watering Can or Hose**—These tools are necessary to provide your plants with the water they need to grow.

**Stakes and String**—You will use these tools to mark the rows in your garden.

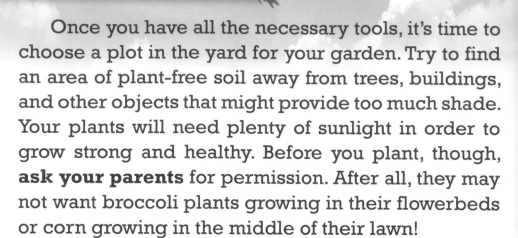

Once you have all the necessary tools, it's time to choose a plot in the yard for your garden. Try to find an area of plant-free soil away from trees, buildings, and other objects that might provide too much shade. Your plants will need plenty of sunlight in order to grow strong and healthy. Before you plant, though, **ask your parents** for permission. After all, they may not want broccoli plants growing in their flowerbeds or corn growing in the middle of their lawn!

The first step in getting the garden space ready is to break up the soil. Imagine how hard it would be for a plant's tender roots and stems to push through rock-hard dirt. It will be much easier for the plant to grow if you loosen the soil before you plant the seeds.

The best tool to use for this task is the hoe. As you strike the soil with the hoe's long, thin blade, remove any weeds and rocks you see. Don't just break up the top crust of the soil. Try to go down into the ground at least 12 inches.

## Garden Tip

*Remember, some plants need more sunlight than others. Look at the back of the seed packet for words such as "full sun," "partial sun," and "shade." You'll need to keep this information in mind when you decide where to plant each type of vegetable.*

Isaac spent several hours hoeing his garden plot. Hoeing helps remove weeds with shallow roots from your garden. It also helps make the soil light and fluffy, so water can seep down deep into it. This will allow your plants to get plenty to drink. Hoeing also helps spread the nutrients around in the soil.

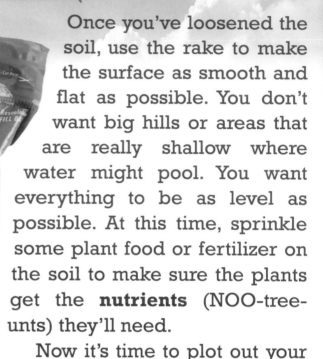

Once you've loosened the soil, use the rake to make the surface as smooth and flat as possible. You don't want big hills or areas that are really shallow where water might pool. You want everything to be as level as possible. At this time, sprinkle some plant food or fertilizer on the soil to make sure the plants get the **nutrients** (NOO-tree-unts) they'll need.

Now it's time to plot out your garden space. The types of plants you've chosen to grow will determine how your garden is arranged. After all, not all plants grow to be the same size and shape. Some plants grow tall, while other plants spread out along the ground.

The best way to figure out how much room each type of vegetable needs is to look again at the back of the seed packets. As you'll see on the broccoli packet, the rows for this vegetable need to be three feet apart, and you should end up with only one plant every two feet. From this information, you can tell that broccoli plants will spread out across the ground, so they'll need lots of room to grow.

The next thing Isaac did in the garden was rake the soil. He wanted to make sure the soil was smooth and the garden plot was level. It is important to do this to your garden so that your plants can grow in nice even rows.

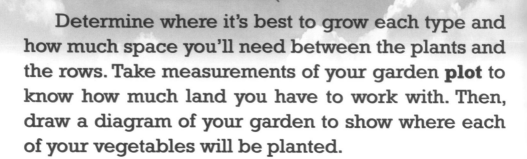

Determine where it's best to grow each type and how much space you'll need between the plants and the rows. Take measurements of your garden **plot** to know how much land you have to work with. Then, draw a diagram of your garden to show where each of your vegetables will be planted.

*Seed packets contain all the information you need to know about the plant. The packet tells you when you should plant the seeds in your area. It tells you how to plant the seeds. It also describes how to take care of the plant after it starts growing, and when you can pick the vegetables. Seed packets are like an encyclopedia article all packed onto one little envelope!*

BROCCOLI
Barbados Hybrid
5426

Gardener's Helpline
1-800-283-3400

Sell by:

This top performing hybrid forms small tight beads on semi-domed heads. Deep, blue-green color. Excellent for fresh use. This packet will plant approximately a 25 foot row.

Directions & Care:
Start seed indoors 6-8 weeks before last killing frost in spring or sow 2-3 seeds together outdoors every 2 feet. Thin to 1 plant every 2 feet when 1 inch tall. Keep watered and fertilized. Cut before buds open for best harvest.

| Days to Germination | 10-14 |
| Days to Harvest | 60-70 |
| Planting Depth | 1/2 in |
| Spacing | Rows 3 ft/Plants 2 ft |
| Seedling ID | |

Uses: Broccoli is a good producer again when planted in summer for fall harvest until frost. For a low calorie dish, broccoli is delicious with lemon juice.

When to Plant:
- April-June
- Mar-Apr & Jun-Jul
- Feb-Mar & Jul-Aug
- July-Dec

0 11192 30347 3

Mfg. by Ferry-Morse Seed Co.
Fulton, KY 42041

Packed for season

RECYCLED PAPER
40% Pre-Consumer Content
10% Post-Consumer Content

*Isaac studied his notes from the garden shop. After he decided which plants to grow in his garden, he mapped out where to plant them.*

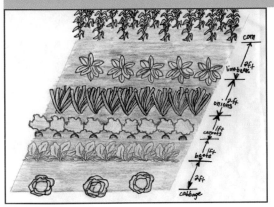

Here's a picture of how Isaac arranged his garden. See how the corn grows taller than any other vegetable? Since he didn't want the tall cornstalks to shade his other plants, he placed them in the back of the garden. (Note: When growing corn, you'll need at least four rows, or they won't make ears.) Isaac also planted fewer cabbage plants than any other vegetable. Why? Cabbage needs lots of room to grow. He also spaced his rows according to the type of vegetable he was growing and its particular needs.

After you've planned your garden, you'll be ready to go on to the next step: planting your seeds.

Chapter *Chapter* **3**

HERBS

# Sowing Seeds

Starting vegetable plants from seeds is one of the best parts about gardening. You get to see how a little seed, after being placed in good soil and given water and sunlight, can grow into a healthy plant. It doesn't matter what age you are, watching tiny plants rise out of the soil is always an amazing experience.

If your growing season is short, you might want to start your plants indoors, planting seeds in individual pots. You'll still get to see them sprout, and once it's warm enough to move them outside, you can **transplant** them into your garden. However, if you need to plant your garden from **seedlings** that you buy, there is still plenty more to enjoy about your garden.

Before you can plant your seeds or seedlings, you have to form rows in the soil. To do this, it's best to start near the edge of the garden and work your way across. Using the hand trowel, make a shallow line in the soil from one end of the garden to the other. This is your first row. Mark it with a stake and label it with the vegetable's name that you want to plant there. Then, according to your diagram, measure the correct distance to the next row.

Make the second row just like you did the first, and mark it with another stake. Keep measuring and marking until all the rows are prepared.

With your garden marked and labeled, you can finally plant your first row of seeds. Let's imagine that you want to plant broccoli in the first row. You would walk along the row, dropping two seeds every two

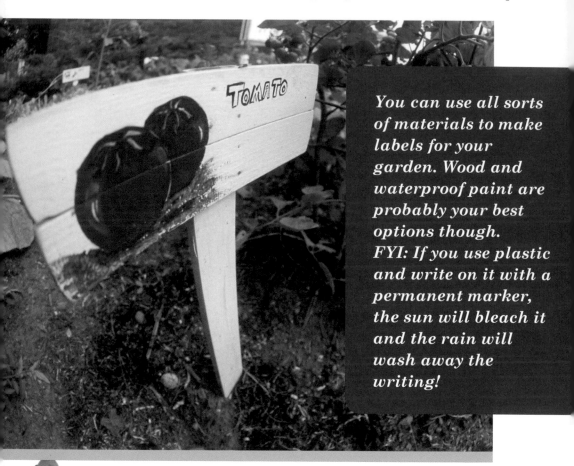

*You can use all sorts of materials to make labels for your garden. Wood and waterproof paint are probably your best options though.*
*FYI: If you use plastic and write on it with a permanent marker, the sun will bleach it and the rain will wash away the writing!*

Along with planting seeds, you can buy plants that have been started or that you have started yourself and plant them in the ground. Here, Isaac is planting some pumpkin plants that he bought at the store.

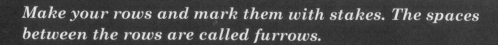

*Make your rows and mark them with stakes. The spaces between the rows are called furrows.*

feet. Remember, this is the distance apart given in the seed packet instructions.

Once you finish dropping the seeds in the row, cover them with soil. Just as different types of seeds need different amounts of room to grow, they also need to be buried in different amounts of soil. This is called planting depth—and this information is also on the back of the seed packet. The broccoli seeds need to be covered with ½ inch of soil.

One way to water your garden is by making furrows between the rows. Furrows are long trenches or ditches. When you place a hose at one end of the furrow, the water will trickle down and form a long river in between your plants. Then the water in the furrows will seep down into the ground and give your plants' roots a healthy drink of water.

After your seeds are planted, you'll need to water your garden. You can use either a watering can to sprinkle water on each row, or you can place a hose at the start of each row and let the water flow gently down to the end. Watering your garden is something you will need to do often. Your plants need water in order to grow, but too much water can be harmful to them. How do you know if you're giving your plants enough water? Just look at the soil each day to see if it is dry. If it is, you'll need to water your garden again. It's best to water during the cooler parts of the day so that the water gets to the roots before it **evaporates** (ee-VAA-por-ayts).

When will your seeds start growing? That all depends on the types of vegetables you planted. Seeds all grow at different rates. For example, you'll see tiny broccoli plants in 10 to 14 days, yet it takes tomato plants only 7 to 10 days to sprout. Other plants might take a couple of weeks before they break the surface of the soil. If you want to know how long it will take for your plants to grow, look at the back of the

## Garden Tip

*If you don't want to plant seeds in your garden, you can also buy the plants directly from the garden shop. One benefit of planting a garden this way is that you'll have vegetables much sooner. The drawback: You'll miss out on watching the seeds turn into plants.*

*You should always space the plants in your garden the correct distance apart. If you don't, the plants will overcrowd each other. They won't be able to get the sunlight and nutrients they need to grow big and strong.*

seed packet again. This time, look for the words *Days to **Germination*** (jer-mih-NAY-shun). This tells you how many days you'll need to wait to see the plants start to grow.

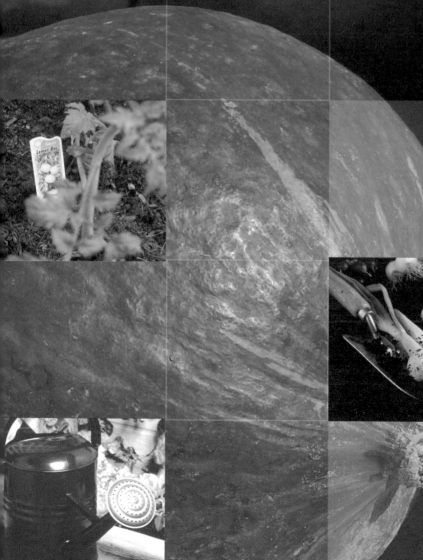

# Harvest Time

Over the next few months, you'll need to take special care of your garden. You'll have to water it often and keep the rows free of weeds. If you are growing beans, you'll have to install a pole on which the vines can climb. If you're growing tomatoes, you'll have to place a cage around the plants so that the fruit will not rest on the ground and rot.

Another thing you'll need to do is make sure your plants do not get eaten by insects. One way people keep insects off their plants is to spray them with **insecticide** (in-SEK-tih-syd). If you decide this is the way you want to keep the pests away, **an adult** will have to do this for you. Insecticide is a poison and can be extremely dangerous if not handled properly.

If you don't want to use a poison to keep the insects off your plants, you can try organic farming. Organic farmers do not like using chemicals to protect their foods from insects. Instead, they use other methods. One is called companion-plant farming. When certain plants are grown side by side, they help each other keep diseases and insects from destroying their fruits. Basil is a companion plant for tomatoes and peppers.

Eggplant is a companion plant for beans and spinach. As you can see from the chart on page 33, there are many plants that help each other in the garden. There are also "bad companions"—plants that harm each other when they are grown close together.

*Some plants, such as pole beans and peas, grow on vines. For these kinds of plants, you'll need to build a trellis or install some poles nearby so that the vines have something on which to climb.*

| Plant | Good Companions | Bad Companions |
|---|---|---|
| Basil | peppers, tomatoes, marigolds | |
| Beans | most herbs and vegetables | onions |
| Cabbage | strong herbs, celery, beets, onions, chamomile, spinach, chard | strawberries, tomatoes, dill |
| Carrots | peas, lettuce, onions, sage, tomatoes | dill |
| Celery | nasturtium, onions, cabbage, tomatoes | |
| Cucumber | beans, peas, sunflowers, radishes | strong herbs, potatoes |
| Eggplant | beans, spinach | |
| Lettuce | carrots, radishes, strawberries, cucumbers | |
| Onions | beets, carrots, lettuce, cabbage | beans, peas |
| Parsley | tomatoes, asparagus | |
| Peas | carrots, radishes, turnips, cucumbers, beans | onions, potatoes |
| Potatoes | beans, cabbage, horseradish, marigolds | sunflowers, cucumbers, tomatoes |
| Radishes | peas, nasturtium, lettuce, cucumbers | hyssop |
| Spinach | strawberries, broad beans | |
| Tomatoes | cabbage, carrots, celery, onions, mint | corn, fennel, potatoes |
| Turnips | peas | potatoes |

After working on your garden every day, you may start to wonder when you'll get the chance to eat some of your tasty vegetables. Once again, the answer to this question is found on the back of your seed packets. When you look at the broccoli packet, for example, you'll see that broccoli takes 60 to 70 days to **mature**. Larger plants generally take much longer

*You can pick carrots when they are small or wait until they have grown to full-size. Just remember that these vegetables grow in the ground, so you need to make sure you wash the dirt off before you eat them!*

CARROTS

It's fun to watch your plants grow from tiny seeds into vegetable-bearing bushes. Isaac watched his pea plants each day. First they developed flowers. Then the flowers turned into tiny pods. It wasn't too much longer before the pods plumped up with little peas growing inside.

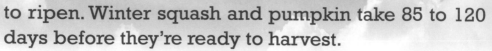

to ripen. Winter squash and pumpkin take 85 to 120 days before they're ready to harvest.

If you chose a variety of vegetables, most likely they will ripen throughout the growing season. It's fun to pick peas one week, zucchini another week, and tomatoes the next.

Chances are, even if you planned well, you'll still harvest more vegetables from your garden than you and your family can eat. If this is the case, maybe you could open your own farmer's stand to sell your extra vegetables. You'll have to ask your parents first for permission, of course. If they think it's a good idea, this might be a great way to earn some extra money. Or, if you don't want to sit all day in the hot sun at a stand selling your crops, perhaps you'd prefer giving your extra vegetables to some neighbors who could use them. Sometimes, food banks and homeless shelters will also take extra produce from people's gardens.

There are plenty of ways that you can store your vegetables. Zucchini can be grated, cooked, and

## Garden Tip

*Do you know why pumpkins are so popular for Halloween and Thanksgiving? They take so long to ripen (85 to 120 days) that they're usually not ready to be picked until the middle or end of autumn.*

*Did you know that you can eat peas right out of the garden? Just snap open a pod and watch the round peas roll into your hand!*

frozen for later use in cookies and cakes. Peas and corn can be canned or frozen. Tomatoes can also be canned. If you decide to do any of these projects, however, you'll definitely need an adult to help you.

# Planting in Small Spaces

Not everyone has a plot of land in which to grow a garden. Many people live in apartment buildings or in crowded cities where backyards are hard to come by. Some people live on boats and don't have any land in which to grow their plants. Does that mean they can't grow their own vegetables? No! People grow gardens in small spaces all the time. If you don't have a backyard, no problem. This chapter will teach you how to grow a garden in pots and other containers.

It is true that if you live in an apartment or on a boat it would probably be very difficult to grow a pumpkin patch. But there are many other plants that you can grow on your balcony, ledge, rooftop, boat deck, or kitchen windowsill.

When you're buying seeds or plants to grow in containers, look for the words *dwarf, bush,* or *miniature* in the plant's name. These words tell you that the plant will not grow very big. For example, you can buy seeds for dwarf tomato plants, small eggplant bushes, and miniature cucumber plants at your local garden shop or, with your parents' permission, over the Internet. All these plants are small enough to be grown in containers. If you live in a warm climate, you can even buy dwarf lemon

*Growing plants in containers is something that people everywhere can enjoy. It doesn't matter how old you are or where you live, you can start your own garden in a pot anytime.*

and orange trees that can be grown in pots on a patio, balcony, or deck.

Follow the same general guidelines when growing plants in containers as you would for growing plants in a garden. First, make sure you provide your plant with good soil and plant food. Next, place your plant in the right-sized container. If you don't give your plant enough space, it won't be able to grow big and strong and produce vegetables. Follow the directions that come with the seeds or plant, and give it the right amount of water. Too little or too much water can kill a plant quickly. The last, yet very important rule, is to make

## Vegetables That Can Be Grown in a Container

| | |
|---|---|
| Beans | Green Onions |
| Beets | Herbs |
| Broccoli | Lettuce |
| Cabbage | Lima Beans |
| Carrots | Peas |
| Cauliflower | Peppers |
| Corn | Radishes |
| Cucumbers | Spinach |
| Eggplants | Tomatoes |

sure you give your plant the right amount of sunlight. Some plants require full sun, others require partial sun, and some like to be in the shade. Placing your plant in the correct location will help it to live longer and produce a good amount of vegetables.

## Garden Tip

*Do you live in a hot climate? If so, avoid using dark-colored containers for your vegetables. These containers will get too hot in the sun, which could harm your plant.*

Look on page 41 for a list of some of the vegetables and herbs that you can grow in containers. Of course, there are many more than what's listed. Ask the garden shop employees for help if you need it. They are experts on the types of plants that are best to grow in your area.

Most people simply use pots to grow their indoor or balcony plants, but these aren't the only containers that you can use. Plants can grow in just about any type of container: metal soup cans, plastic drinking cups, pails, buckets, tubs, baskets, and troughs. Some people have even used old shoes, tires, and plastic beach balls cut in half to house their plants! The one important feature of all these containers is that they have holes in the bottom of them. This allows extra water to drain. Without the holes, your plant could get moldy and die. If your container doesn't

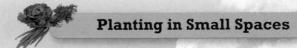

*You can grow vegetables and herbs, such as chives and rosemary, indoors or outside.*

have holes, you can ask someone to drill or poke the holes in it for you.

Now you can no longer use the excuse that you don't have a backyard for not starting a garden. Just about anyone can grow some type of plant, no matter where they live.

There's nothing quite like walking into a backyard garden or a home filled with plants. Visitors feel a sense of peace and relaxation, and the gardener feels a sense of pride at taking an important role in helping care for Earth's natural resources. Gardening is definitely a hobby in which the earth and all its inhabitants can benefit. So what are you waiting for? Get started today on your new hobby of gardening.

## Hummingbird Bath

Birds, bees, and other insects are very important for a garden. They help **pollinate** (PAH-lih-nayt) a plant's flowers so that it can produce fruit and vegetables.

Hummingbirds are one type of bird that pollinates. To attract these kinds of birds to your garden, you can set up a bird bath. You can buy one from the store, or you could make one very easily out of a carrot.

**You Will Need**
An adult
Kitchen knife
Carrot—about 8 inches long and 1.5 inches thick
Vegetable peeler
Bamboo skewer
Scissors
Red yarn

**Tips**
* Ask your parents to help you with the first step!
* Add red flowers or other red decorations to your bird bath. Hummingbirds are attracted to the color red.

## Directions

1. **Ask an adult** to cut an inch off the top of a thick carrot.

2. Have the adult help you use the tip of a vegetable peeler to make a well in the top of the carrot. The well will later be filled with water. Keep drilling until the well is about two inches deep and one inch wide.

3. Push a bamboo skewer through the well, about an inch down from the top. Center your carrot on the skewer.

4. Cut a piece of red yarn. Tie the ends to each end of the skewer to make a loop. (You can also simply use the skewer to thread the yarn through the holes.)

5. Hang your carrot bird bath on a tree branch or on a stick or post near your garden.

6. Carefully fill the well in the carrot with water.

7. Watch for hummingbird visitors. It won't be long before they come to get a refreshing drink of water from your bird bath!

# Further Reading

**Books**

Bradley, Clare. *Fun With Gardening: 50 Great Projects Kids Can Plant Themselves.* London: Southwater Publishing, 2000.

Krezel, Cindy. *Kids Container Gardening: Year-Round Projects for Inside and Out.* Batavia, Illinois: Ball Publishing, 2005.

Morris, Karyn. *Jumbo Book of Gardening (Kids Can Press Jumbo Books).* Minneapolis, Minnesota: Tandem Library Books, 2000.

Rushing, Felder. *Dig, Plant, Grow: A Kid's Guide to Gardening.* Nashville, Tennessee: Cool Springs Press, 2004.


**Web Sites For Kids**

How to Grow Corn
    http://www.ehow.com/how_1997_grow-corn.html

National Gardening Association: Kids Gardening
    http://www.kidsgardening.com/

University of Illinois Extension: My First Garden
    http://www.urbanext.uiuc.edu/firstgarden/


**Works Consulted**

Atha, Antony. *The Container Kitchen Garden.* New York: Collins & Brown, 2000.

Bartholomew, Mel. *Square Foot Gardening.* Emmaus, Pennsylvania: Rodale Press, 1981.

Donaldson, Stephanie. *The Ultimate Container Gardener.* New York: Lorenz Books, 1999.

Guerra, Michael. *The Edible Container Garden.* New York: Fireside, 2000.

McCausland, Jim. "Summer Veggies in Pots." *Sunset,* March 2001. http://www.sunset.com/sunset/garden/article/0,20633,767744,00.html

McCausland, Jim. "These Tasty Crops Thrive in Pots." *Sunset,* April 2003. http://www.sunset.com/sunset/garden/article/0,20633,681427,00.html

Peel, Lucy. *Kitchen Garden: What to Grow and How to Grow It.* New York: Harper Collins, 2003.

Riotte, Louise. *Carrots Love Tomatoes.* North Adams, Massachusetts: Story Publishing, LLC., 1998.

Swezey, Lauren Bonar. "Grow a Veggie Garden in Pots." *Sunset,*
    April 2004. http://www.sunset.com/sunset/garden/
    article/0,20633,677661,00.html

**On the Internet**
Alabama Cooperative Extension System:
    http://www.aces.edu/pubs/docs/A/ANR-1041/
Better Homes and Gardens
    http://www.bhg.com/bhg/gardening/index.jsp
Garden Guides, Your Guide to Everything Garden
    http://www.gardenguides.com/
Home & Garden Television Online
    http://www.hgtv.com/hgtv/gardening/
National Gardening Association
    http://www.garden.org
Sunset Magazine Online
    http://www.sunset.com/sunset/

# Glossary

**climate** (KLY-met)—The usual weather patterns for an area.

**edible** (EH-dih-bul)—Safe for eating.

**evaporates** (ee-VAA-por-ayts)—Turns from a liquid into a gas.

**germination** (jer-mih-NAY-shun)—The process seeds go through when they start to grow.

**insecticide** (in-SEK-tih-syd)—Chemicals or poisons that are used to kill insects.

**mature** (muh-CHOOR)—Fully grown.

**nutrients** (NOO-tree-unts)—Things in food or soil that help animals and plants grow strong and healthy.

**plot**—A small area of ground for planting.

**pollinate** (PAH-lih-nayt)—Transfer parts of one flower to another so that the plant can make a fruit or vegetable.

**seedling**—A young plant or tree grown from a seed.

**transplant** (TRANS-plant)—To move a plant from one plot of soil to another.

**zone** (ZOHN)—An area in which particular plants and animals can live at certain times of the year.

# Index

**Photo Credits:** Cover, pp. 6–7, 9, 14–15, 22–23, 24, 30–31, 32, 33, 34, 37, 38–39, 40, 41, 44—Jupiter Images; pp. 1, 2–3, 4–5, 6, 10, 11, 12, 17, 19, 20, 21, 25, 26, 27, 29, 35, 43, 45, 44–48 (background)—Amie Jane Leavitt.